Learning to Read with Ladybird

A guide for parents and carers

Contents

About this book

This book will:

show you how to encourage your child's love of books and reading, from babyhood to first years at school

explain how children are currently taught to read – the synthetic phonics method

give you ideas for supporting this method at home

show you how Ladybird's reading schemes can help your child to learn to read.

Star tips to encourage reading

✳ Show your child how much **you** enjoy reading.

✳ Have lots of books and reading materials in your home.

✳ Show you are pleased with what your child achieves and try not to hurry each stage.

✳ Keep sessions short – ten minutes with books a day is fine.

✳ Keep up the bedtime story!

Begin at the beginning – babies and books

From early days, babies are learning to:

communicate – when he's a few days old, he'll know your voice, and before he's eight weeks old, he'll be speaking to you in his own way, with a gurgle or a coo*

touch and look – he'll be using his senses to understand the world around him, and focusing on more and more detail

explore – curiosity is one of the strongest drivers in learning

talk – he'll make sounds that come closer and closer to speech. Talking is our fundamental life-skill so it's especially important to make time to talk

listen – you can encourage this vital skill. Have fun making noises and talk to your baby about the different sounds you hear

store up words – children need to build up a mental store of the names for different objects and these will be among the first words they will need for reading.

*although we have used the word 'he' here, the advice in this book is suitable for boys and girls.

Encourage your child by:

singing nursery rhymes with a colourful picture rhyme book

letting your baby play with the pages of books. (This is what he thinks you are doing!)

4

Nursery rhymes are important

✳ They boost language development, awareness of sound, and imagination.

✳ They help young children to understand sequence and story.

✳ They are zany, visual and fun.

✳ They are full of the repetition babies and toddlers need to hear so that they can begin to anticipate what's coming, and eventually join in.

✳ They are part of our literary and childhood heritage – and encourage the vital social aspect of reading. It's magical for children to realize that lots of important people know the same rhymes that they do.

Getting the best from stories

* Read stories every day, at different times and in different places.

* Talk about the story before and afterwards with your child.

* Talk about the detail in the pictures – does the princess look excited? What do you think is going to happen now?

* Match something in the story to your child's experience; for example, 'You were hungry, too, after that long walk, weren't you?'

Stepping up – toddlers

Older babies and toddlers need lots of variety in their books.

Young children love story and picture books and they have firm favourites – often with animal characters, such as Peppa Pig.

This is a very ME time, so look for simple books which focus on the world of young children, their favourite things and their first experiences. Story books and books that list simple facts are ideal.

Books which encourage curiosity and touch are great for getting young children involved – textured books, noisy books, lift the flap books!

Baby Touch
Peekaboo

Noisy Noisy
Nee-Naw!

Toddler
Play and Say
Big!
A little book of opposites

Getting ready to read

Encouraging your child

Allow her plenty of time for play, stories, rhymes and songs.

Make opportunities to talk and listen, and to use lots of new words.

Enjoy favourite books together – read and talk: bedtime story is best of all.

Say and sing nursery rhymes together.

Play listening games – put a collection of small noisy objects into a bag: keys, squeaky toys, two spoons, coins. Keep the objects hidden – and ask your child what the noise is!

Play spot the difference games – these are great for concentration and for looking at details: remember that print is all about small details!

Ready-to-read checklist

In order to begin real reading,
your child needs to be able to:

✳ enjoy sharing stories and talking
   about them

✳ concentrate for a short time

✳ understand that words are different
   from pictures

✳ recognize and distinguish sounds

✳ look at small details and see
   differences between them

✳ understand how books work.

Words and pictures

A big step towards reading is to understand
that words are different from pictures.
At first, children see words as black patterns
on the page. Explain that these patterns are
words and that they tell you what to say –
it's the words that tell you the story. Say that
one day, when she can read, the words will
tell her what to say, too.

How books work

When you share a book,
your child will learn:

how to hold a book

that the outside of a book is different from the inside

that the pictures are full of interesting things and are the
same each time she sees them

that we keep the book still and turn the pages

that a story in a particular book says the same each time

that books come 'with' you and other important people,
and mean exciting times together.

The synthetic phonics approach to reading

Phonics teaches children the link between letters and the sounds they make. This is called the **alphabetic code.**

When we talk, our words are made up of different sounds. **Synthetic phonics** links these sounds with their letter shapes when they are written down.

Children are taught how sounds and letter shapes go together to make the words we read. When they begin to learn to read, children will be using synthetic phonics to work out what the words say.

They will learn to break the word into parts and sound the parts out. This is called **segmenting**. They will then put them back together, and this is called **blending**.

An example of blending is:

t + a + p = tap

In the UK, children are taught to read using a structured synthetic phonics method. Most children will begin a synthetic phonics programme by the age of five. The aim is that they should become fluent readers and be able to read words automatically by the age of seven.

Letter names or sounds?

* We use letter **sounds** when we talk about the little letters in words: **a** as in **a**pple, **b** as in **b**us, **c** as in **c**at. The **phonics** approach is about the use of these letters and sounds.

* We use letter **names** in the capital letter alphabet: **A B C**. Being able to use these names is helpful for children's spelling.

* Children will learn both letter sounds and letter names when they start learning to read.

Pre-school synthetic phonics

How can you help with the synthetic phonics approach at home?

The first step is to help your child to notice the differences between sounds. Nursery rhymes and songs are full of opportunities to hear rhyming sounds and funny sound effects. Add your own **quacks**, **baas**, **bangs**, **sizzles** and **pops**.

Go on a listening walk through the house. **Shhh – really listen hard. What can you hear?**

Play games about sounds. *I spy with my little eye* focuses on sounds at the beginning of words. Use the letter sound (**d** as in **dog**). ***I spy with my little eye something beginning with d…***

Go on a different sound hunt each day. Draw a **t** and say, '***Let's go on a t hunt today. What can we see that begins with the sound t***?' Examples are: **tap**, **television**, **teddy**, **teapot**, **table**, **telephone**.

Teach your child alphabet names (**A B C**) by singing the alphabet. Any tune will do! Write it out in order using capital letters, or use a colourful capital letter alphabet book and look at the order of the alphabet as you sing.

My first rhymes

A collection of traditional rhymes to sing, say and share. young babies and toddlers will love the colour and fun of Ladybird's My First Rhymes.

Jack and Jill

Jack and Jill went up the hill
To fetch a pail of water.
Jack fell down and broke his crown
And Jill came tumbling after.

Synthetic phonics at school

When children are on the synthetic phonics programme at school they will:

learn that letters have sounds that go with them

learn to listen to the individual sounds in words, and match them with their written letter shapes

practise being able to sound out more and more words

learn more and more sounds associated with letters

learn to read some very useful words by sight. Some words are hard to decode in the early stages of phonic learning because their letters are not pronounced in the most obvious way. These are often referred to as 'tricky words'. For example:

the   to   be   said

In phonics, sounds are called **phonemes**.

Written letter shapes are called **graphemes**.

Sometimes teachers use these words in class, so your child may know them.

The 44 phonemes

These are the sounds that make up the English language. One example spelling is given for each sound.

Consonant phonemes:	Vowel phonemes:
b as in **b**un	**a** as in **a**pple
c as in **c**up	**e** as in **e**gg
d as in **d**og	**i** as in **i**t
f as in **f**rog	**o** as in **o**n
g as in **g**o	**u** as in **u**p
h as in **h**en	**ai** as in r**ai**n
j as in **j**et	**ee** as in f**ee**t
l as in **l**ip	**igh** as in r**igh**t
m as in **m**op	**oa** as in b**oa**t
n as in **n**et	**oo** as in b**oo**t
p as in **p**ip	**oo** as in l**oo**k
r as in **r**un	**ow** as in c**ow**
s as in **s**ip	**oi** as in j**oi**n
t as in **t**op	**ar** as in f**ar**m
v as in **v**an	**or** as in f**or**
w as in **w**ig	**ur** as in h**ur**t
y as in **y**es	**air** as in f**air**
z as in **z**ip	**ear** as in n**ear**
sh as in **sh**ip	**ure** as in s**ure**
ch as in **ch**at	**u** as in corn**u**
th as in **th**in	
th as in **th**en	
ng as in ri**ng**	
zh as in vi**si**on	

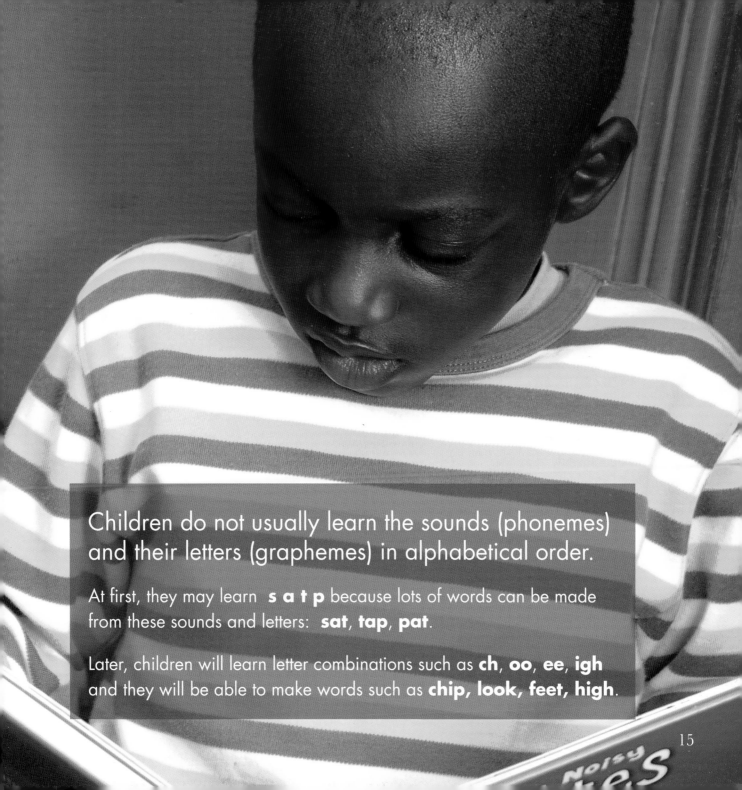

Children do not usually learn the sounds (phonemes) and their letters (graphemes) in alphabetical order.

At first, they may learn **s a t p** because lots of words can be made from these sounds and letters: **sat**, **tap**, **pat**.

Later, children will learn letter combinations such as **ch**, **oo**, **ee**, **igh** and they will be able to make words such as **chip, look, feet, high**.

How to help at home

Ask your child's teacher how she would like you to help.

Carry on sharing books – especially the bedtime story.

Make six cards with lower case consonants on them, one on each. Choose letters and sounds that your child has learned, for example: **s**, **t**, **p**, **n**.

Make cards with the five vowels on them – **a e i o u** – one on each.

See how many three letter words with vowels in the middle you can make.

Some examples of CVC [consonant/vowel /consonant] words are:
bed man top pig hut

tip
pan
pin
sit
nip

Consonants:
bcdfghjklmn
pqrstvwxyz
Vowels:
a e i o u

As your child learns more letters and more sounds, make more cards and more words!

You may need to make more than one card of some letters so that you can make words with double letters such as **rabbit**.

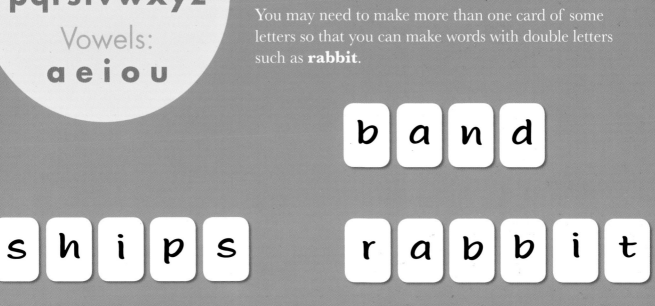

band

ships   **rabbit**

Alphabetic fridge magnet are great! You and your child can make a word a day with the letters she has learned. Can you make sentences together using the words your child has learned to read?

we pat the dog

It's useful for children to see a written letter shape at the same time as they learn and say the sound. See if your child's teacher can tell you the way that handwriting is taught at school, and follow the same way of forming the letters.

Phonics with Ladybird

For children who have completed their initial phonic learning and are eager to read exciting stories!

Ladybird's Superhero Phonic Readers are:

* a new, exciting series of stories designed to draw children into the wider world of reading

* perfect for the stage when children have completed their initial phonic learning and are ready to read books with an increasingly wide vocabulary

* designed to support the phonics method by having a high number of words that can be read this way

* progressive and confidence building

* planned to develop children's concentration and understanding in exciting ways

* about real reading, real stories, real meaning, real progress!

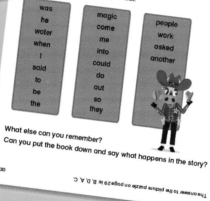

"Thanks, Jade," say the police.
"You helped us to catch Dax Doom."

Thanks, Jade.

And now Dax Doom is safely be...
Or is he?

27

...er these words from the story?
...You can read them super-fast.

was	magic	people
he	come	work
water	me	asked
when	into	another
I	could	
said	do	
to	out	
be	so	
the	they	

What else can you remember?
Can you put the book down and say what happens in the story?

30

The answer to the picture puzzle on page 29 is: B, D, A, C.

Ask an adult to cut this page out for you. You can stick it on your wall.

I'm a phonic
Superhero

I can read all of *Cow Boy*.

I can read all the tricky words.

By _____

Date _____

31

Contains:
Parent notes
Puzzle pages
Reward chart
Stickers

Superhero
Phonic Readers
The Cat in the Mask
level 1

Superhero
Phonic Readers
Zain Zoom
level 2

Superhero
Phonic Readers
Jumping Jade
level 3

Superhero
Phonic Readers
Cow Boy
level 4

Superhero
Phonic Readers
X-Ray Rex
level 5

Superhero
Phonic Readers
Invisible Liz
level 6

Superhero
Phonic Readers
The Super Twins
level 7

Superhero
Phonic Readers
Super Robot
level 8

Superhero
Phonic Readers
Stella Stone
level 9

Superhero
Phonic Readers
The Super Reader
level 10

19

Ladybird's Key Words with Peter and Jane

This is Ladybird's classic, tried-and-tested reading scheme based on the most frequently occurring words in our language.

It can be helpful and confidence building for children to recognize these key words on sight. Examples are: *the*, *one*, *two*, *he*. Many of these occur very often in reading material. The structured repetition of these words in Key Words with Peter and Jane ensures reading fluency.

The scheme is clear, straightforward and very thorough indeed.

The girl has some cards. Each card has a picture on it.

She looks at the picture on each card and puts it with the letter sound.

There are pictures of a boy, a cat, a top, an apple, a fish, a hat, a man, and the sun.

The letter sounds are **b, c, t, a, f, h, m,** and **s.**

Sounds we know from Book 4c

See notes

Peter is here
and
Jane is here.

Read it yourself

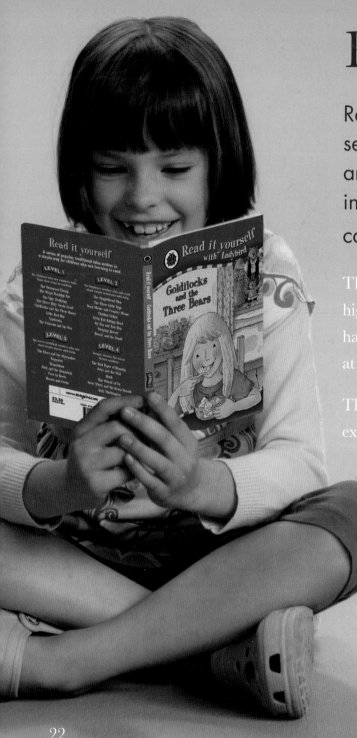

Read it yourself is Ladybird's classic series featuring traditional stories that are are part of every child's literary inheritance. And, best of all, children can read each one for themselves!

The stories are carefully structured to include many high frequency words, and are great for children who have completed their phonic focus in their first year at school.

There are four levels of stories, with clearly explained progression.

Although written simply and with repetition, the stories are rich in content and meaning, and the repetition is part of the story.

The series is illustrated using a variety of styles to motivate the reader, aid progress and promote success!

A fairy godmother came to Cinderella's house. She made Cinderella a beautiful dress. She made Cinderella some beautiful shoes.

12